THE WILD SIDE

PERSONAL BOOKLET

Life JOURNEYS

Published 2007 by CWR, Waverley Abbey House, Waverley Lane, Farnham, Surrey GU9 8EP, UK.
Registered Charity No. 294387.
Registered Limited Company No. 1990308.
Reprinted 2008, 2009 and 2010.
Bible reading notes included in this booklet previously published by CWR in the September/October 2005 issue of *Lucas on Life Every Day*, by Jeff Lucas.

Introduction: Andy Peck. Questions for group discussion: Jeff Lucas and Andy Peck.

For a list of our National Distributors visit www.cwr.org.uk/distributors

Concept development, editing, design and production by CWR
Printed in the UK by Bishops Printers
ISBN: 978-1-85345-439-4

DAILY READINGS: **JEFF LUCAS**
GROUP DISCUSSION QUESTIONS:
JEFF LUCAS AND ANDY PECK

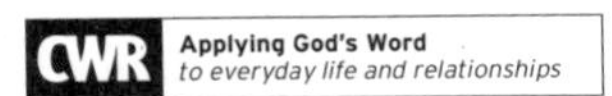

CONTENTS

INTRODUCTION

Jonah – wasn't he the guy who was swallowed by a whale? The disobedient prophet who eventually got his act together? Well yes and no. We think we know the details of the story, but there's so much more. Firstly, it was a large fish, not a whale, and secondly, it wasn't all glory for the prophet at the end.

Jeff Lucas takes a fresh look at a familiar story and shows us that as well as a man being eaten by a large fish, the book of Jonah has many more striking images. There's Jonah the marathon runner; a storm that provokes seasoned mariners to scream; a whole city in revival; a fast-growing plant; and a worm that ruins Jonah's day.

But the most vivid image is that of God Himself. However fast Jonah ran, God ran faster, relentlessly – and lovingly – pursuing him. Here we see a God who could have rained down fire and brimstone on Nineveh – and rebellious Jonah – but who instead reached out in kindness to both.

The story of Jonah is not just about an errant prophet and a fish with indigestion, but about a God who is intimately involved in our world – indeed, a God who is intimately involved in your world too. It's time to get to know Him better.

For group leaders ...

How to use

This resource is designed to include all you will need for four small-group sessions. It comprises four DVD clips, group discussion questions based on each clip and Bible readings to be used between each session.

PREPARATION

1. Watch the DVD clip before the meeting.

2. Use the icebreaker to get folk chatting. Select the questions that you think would be most useful for your group to look at. You may want to use them all, depending on the time you have available. We suggest you plan for 30–45 minutes.

THE SESSION

1. Play the DVD clip first and go straight into the icebreaker question.

2. Use the questions you have selected.

3. Move from discussion into prayer. There's a prayer included in the material which you could finish with at the end.

4. Encourage the group to use the daily readings in the days between sessions. The readings expand and build on the topics covered in the DVD. If the group members are not used to daily Bible reading, encourage them to develop this habit. If the group members are already into a routine of Bible reading and prayer each day you might want to discuss how best to work these new readings into their time.

5. You could start the next session by reviewing how the group found the daily readings. What did they learn? Do they have questions to raise? How did God speak?

Session 1:
The Passionate God

ICEBREAKER:

Who's the most passionate person you can think of, either known to you personally, or in the media?

FOR GROUP DISCUSSION:

- How would you define the word 'passion'?
- When you hear that God is passionate – what comes to mind?
- If you were to rate how you perceive God right now, where 1 is remote and 10 is intimately involved, what score would you give?
- Jonah is surprised that God is interested in Assyria. Who in your community would God be calling you to reach, but, frankly, you'd rather not? What problems or challenges might you face in reaching 'those' people?
- Is your church a 'cathedral of passion'? Is passion about volume of noise and outward expressions of enthusiasm?

- Can you think of a time when someone in your church was passionate about something? What was your reaction to this?

- How do you 'hang in there' when you are involved in serving God in an area of ministry, but feel tired and exhausted?

- Has the surprising God surprised you lately?

PRAYER:

Living God,
we thank You that Your heart burns with love
for all that you have made.
You are the God who entwines Himself with our lives,
the One moved by our cares,
and the One who reaches out still
to those who are rejected, despised, or just forgotten.
Open our eyes to see as You see.
Grant us passion, mingled with faithfulness,
that we might go wherever You send us.
In Your name, we pray.
Amen.

A FRIEND who was feeling tired and depressed summed it all up recently; 'My get up and go got up and went', he lamented. Something similar can happen in our spiritual lives. Our initial willingness to go anywhere and do anything for God settles down into a mediocre plod. We embrace a false Christianity that is simply warm and comfortable, where God tucks us up in the silk sheets of our own preferences and Jesus is the fulfiller of our wildest hopes and dreams. He becomes more Santa than Saviour.

But God is disruptive. *He* has a wild dream, and invites us to participate in His kingdom master plan. That might mean that our 'best laid plans' need to take a back seat. The Christian is one who deliberately places themselves under orders, for life.

A ticket to the big city of Nineveh was never on Jonah's wish list. Suddenly he hears 'Go' – in the Hebrew, literally, 'Get up and go'. Both Elijah and Jeremiah heard exactly the same command (1 Kings 17:9; Jer. 13:6).

Jonah may well have rationalised as he wriggled – and then ran in the opposite direction. He may have protested that to be an international prophetic postman was not his ministry; an excuse often used in Christian circles, where what we've done in the past becomes a secure bunker to prevent us from doing anything costly in the present. But God is still the sending God. Are we still willing for our warm, cosy nest to be stirred?

Prayer: Lord, save me from settling. I deliberately place myself under Your direction again today. Use me. Amen.

SESSION 1: DAY 1

Get up and go

BIG PICTURE:
Jonah 1:2
Matthew 8:1–22

FOCUS:
'Go to the great city of Nineveh …' (Jonah 1:2)

… God … invites us to participate in His kingdom master plan

SESSION 1: DAY 2

Tears and sending

BIG PICTURE:
Jonah 1:2
Hosea 11:1–11

FOCUS:
'... preach against it, because its wickedness has come up before me.' (Jonah 1:2)

IT SEEMS almost every day there are images in the news that make us want to weep. The Asian tsunami destroyed so many lives – and, for some, challenged their faith in a good God. Dr Rowan Williams, Archbishop of Canterbury, commented at the time: 'The question, "How can you believe in a God who permits suffering on this scale?" is very much around at the moment …'

Bombarded by images of devastation, we can be tempted to believe that God is dispassionate and detached from it all. But God is the involved One – who sees the suffering, wickedness and injustice in Nineveh, which was why Jonah was conscripted in the first place.

God is not some megalomaniac general who shunts soldiers around the world map like a calculating chess player. A better translation of the word 'preach' in Jonah 1:2 is 'cry to'.

The missionary God cries for His world. In the very last verse of the book of Jonah, God poses the question, 'Should I not be concerned about that great city?' (4:11) – and the word 'concerned' means literally 'to have tears in one's eyes'. This startling portrait of the weeping God is one that we meet again in the pages of the New Testament, as Jesus weeps over the city of Jerusalem (Matt. 23:37) and empathises with Mary's pain over her dead brother Lazarus (John 11:35).

He agonises over His world and suffers with our suffering. Hosea prophesied about a God whose heart 'churns' within Him over His people, who 'provoked' and 'grieved' Him (Hosea 11:8; Psa. 78:40–41, NKJV).

God calls because He cries.

The missionary God cries for His world

Prayer: Lord, help me to sense Your tears when I find myself weeping over injustice and pain. Weep through me. Amen.

Another life

BIG PICTURE:
Jonah 1:3
Romans 1:18–32

FOCUS:
'But Jonah ran away from the LORD ...'
(Jonah 1:3)

IN THE poignant film *American Beauty*, Kevin Spacey plays a tired, depressed man. Overwhelmed by tedium, he is hungry to escape the humdrum. One line of dialogue reveals the profound sorrow in his soul: 'In a year I'll be dead. But in a way, I'm dead already.'

Get a life – or so the saying goes. Perhaps there are times when we'd like to do just that – trade in our current existence and get *another life*. We can be tempted to daydream and fantasise about escaping the daily grind, fleeing the familiar landmarks – even getting away from God, from the moral and spiritual demands of being Christian – although the truth has been 'made plain to us' (see Rom. 1:19). We all have times when we'd like to join the escape committee and break out of what has come to feel like a prison camp.

Our video game/entertainment/leisure culture flourishes because of our hankering to get away, even into unreality. Many marriages break down, not because of cataclysmic conflict, but as a result of the devastating erosion that boredom brings. Exciting fresh pastures beckon. Jonah actually did the proverbial 'runner'. Unwilling to prophesy to the hated Assyrians, he declared rebellion against God and hotfooted to Tarshish – 1,500 miles in the opposite direction of Nineveh. Commanded to go northeast, he went southwest. It's a shocking sight, as we see him bunching his fists against the Lord and the chaos in his life that results.

Perhaps you're on the run – or considering taking a similar trip. Think again before you buy that ticket.

Prayer: Lord, help me to dream, without getting into daydreaming or unhelpful fantasy. Thank You for the reality that is today and that You are with me in it. Amen.

The perfect storm and passion

BIG PICTURE:
Jonah 1:4
Matthew 25:14–30

FOCUS:
'Then the LORD sent a great wind on the sea …' (Jonah 1:4)

GOD is not fobbed off easily. The fugitive prophet's cruise away from his calling turned into a battle for survival, as a great storm overwhelmed the ship – the language in the Hebrew text paints a picture of God 'hurling' the storm at the ship in the same way that a spear is thrown. Although God may have the *weather* firmly under control (Psa. 135:7), *people* can sometimes offer more resistance.

So why did God insist on pursuing Jonah? If the runaway wasn't interested in accepting the Nineveh assignment, then presumably there were others who would step forward to become God's ambassador to the Assyrians …

But Jonah was the chosen instrument for this job. God was passionate in His concern for the wayward citizens of Nineveh. His calling is not for us to complete mere projects, but to participate with Him in reaching and caring for much loved human beings.

The Lord was determined that Jonah should be a man of destiny. Even though the moment was overshadowed by anger, Jonah was being steered by God to walk into his finest hour – the exhilaration of seeing an entire city, from the king down, turn to the Lord. Each one of us was designed for purpose. God invites us, not merely to chase after our small dreams, but to play our unique part in His kingdom plan.

God cares deeply that we reach our potential. Our reluctance to serve Him doesn't create a mere raised eyebrow in heaven, but a wounded heart. He doesn't easily take 'No' for an answer.

> God cares deeply that we reach our potential

Prayer: Father, I want to learn to really live. What plans have You written over my life? Amen.

SESSION 1: DAY 5

A twist in the tale

BIG PICTURE:
Jonah 1:1–17
Ephesians 3:14–21

FOCUS:
'But the LORD provided a great fish to swallow Jonah ...' (Jonah 1:17)

I LOVE surprising endings.

I enjoy those final 'twists' in a film or a book, when something shocking unfolds. It might sound a little irreverent, but as we see a fish under command literally showing up out of the blue to rescue Jonah, we realise that our God really is a shocker.

One moment, Jonah is in mid-air above the mountainous waves – catapulted overboard by those tearful sailors – and suddenly he is safe. When he went over the side, he was a man facing certain death. The grace period for his rebellion had run out, or so he thought, and as he hit the water there was only terror as the waves immediately overwhelmed him. Perhaps he bobbed back to the surface for a moment and screamed out a final, exhausted prayer. In a storm like this, it would be just seconds before he would succumb. Never in his wildest dreams could he have imagined a rescue bid. He was nowhere near land; the sailors had tried to row there, without success.

But everything turns around in a moment for the dead man swimming, as a missionary fish shows up for lunch. Perhaps Jonah caught a glimpse of the huge fish (which commentators say may have been a large shark) approaching him, mouth wide open. The notion that a predator could be his rescuer wouldn't have occurred to him.

But that's the way God is. Grace really is amazing. Can't figure it out? Accept it, like a life belt – or a passing fish – to a drowning man.

Prayer: Forgive me for boxing You in, Lord. Surprise me today. Amen.

Session 2:
Life After Failure

ICEBREAKER:

Can you think of someone, perhaps in public life, who was given a second chance? How did you feel about it?

FOR GROUP DISCUSSION:

- Martin Luther said, 'Most Christians have enough religion to feel guilty about their sin, but not enough to enjoy life in the Spirit.' Why does this happen?

- Jonah did the exact opposite of what God wanted. Have you ever knowingly done that? What happened?

- Repentance starts today. Why do we procrastinate?

- 'God is bigger than our sin.' What sins do we think of as 'big' and more difficult to be forgiven of?

- Jonah's repentance came during a crisis. Can you think of occasions in your life when a crisis caused you to turn back to God?

- When we realise we have sinned we can feel it is not right for God to forgive us and so we wallow in the unpleasantness of it all. How does repentance give us a genuinely clean start? (See Psa. 103:11–12; 2 Cor. 7:10.)

- How can the conscience help us?

- What is the difference between piety and obedience?

Prayer:

Loving God,
For hope after defeat, we thank You.
For cleansing after our moments and seasons of shame, we thank You.
For wisdom that exposes our follies, we thank You.
For grace that is bigger than our sin, we thank You.
For Your hug of welcome that is so undeserved, we give You praise.
Amen.

SESSION 2: DAY 1

Repentance – something good

BIG PICTURE:
Jonah 2:1
Psalm 51:1–19

FOCUS:
'From inside the fish Jonah prayed to the LORD his God.'
(Jonah 2:1)

THE fading bumper sticker says, 'Smile, God loves you.' But there's more to the Christian message than a call to grin about grace. The love of God will at times provoke us to tears. Repentance is at the very heart of New Testament Christianity.

When John the Baptist, the odd chap with strange fashion choices (and a weirder diet), appeared, his opening words were a call to true penitence that was backed up by the fruit of a changed lifestyle (Matt. 3:8). And when Jesus began to preach, His opening message called for a U-turn: 'Repent, for the kingdom of heaven is near' (Matt. 4:17). Repentance is not negative; on the contrary, it's part of the good news, as a bridge to life (Acts 11:18) and freedom that opens up our horizon to a brighter future.

God wants us to be a people of repentance, not because He is a killjoy, but because He cares. So Paul shows us that 'God's *kindness* leads you towards repentance' (Rom. 2:4, my italics).

And it begins today. The gut of a fish is an odd chapel, but it worked well enough for Jonah, and he begins a repentance of sorts – scholars are divided about how sincere he was. And, as he cries, dawn appears in his story. If God is gently prompting us about changes in our lives, let's not wait for a better time or a better place before we respond. However low we've gone, and however deep we find ourselves entrenched in the mess we've made, there's a way back.

God wants us to be people of repentance ...

Prayer: Where sin has hardened me, take me on a journey of renewed repentance, Lord. Amen.

SESSION 2: DAY 2

The school of hard knocks

BIG PICTURE:
Jonah 2:2
Luke 15:11–24

FOCUS:
'In my distress I called to the LORD, and he answered me.' (Jonah 2:2)

JONAH was a tough nut to crack. Entombed in darkness for 72 hours, and probably feeling close to death, he could have lost his mind – but instead, like the prodigal son, he came to his senses. He re-establishes communication with the Lord. Distress was the unwelcome teacher that drove him home to God's heart.

Some of us have to tread hard pathways before we learn the lessons of life. When I was speaking with a minister whose son had been jailed for drug peddling, he and his wife wept as they recounted their decision not to bail him out, feeling that it was more faithful to let him face the consequences of his lifestyle. They could have spared him discomfort, but deprived him of a vital lesson. Like Jonah, that young man finally got tired of a life without God and made a radical decision to live for Christ.

It's surely the hardest prayer to pray, but there are situations where we need to ask God to do whatever it takes to bring someone back to Him. That doesn't mean that we wish people harm, or stop loving or practically caring for them, but to allow someone dear to us to learn that you can't run away from the outcome of your actions may be a great act of love.

When those prodigals yell for help, God instantly hears. Unlike the pious ramblings of the Pharisees, which, figuratively speaking, cause God's eyes to glaze over (Matt. 6:7), He immediately responds to the cry of those who decide they want Him.

Prayer: Lord, when people I love make huge mistakes, redeem those moments. May distress be a teacher, rather than a destroyer of hope. Amen.

Exposing deception

BIG PICTURE:
Jonah 2:4
James 1:19–27

FOCUS:
'I said, "I have been banished from your sight …"' (Jonah 2:4)

THE frequent-flier madness that occasionally takes over my life means that there are times when I wake up in the middle of the night in a hotel and, as I peer up at the ceiling, for a few moments have no idea which country I am in. Jet lag has disorientated me, temporarily disabling my memory and the darkened room offers me no clue. I don't even know where the light switch is. More than once I have felt my way around the walls so I can flip the switch and check my location.

A steadfast commitment to sin will always produce something similar to that in our lives. Deception is married to rebellion, and when we join Jonah on a jog away from God we end up losing our ability to see straight. And that deception is a thick fog that is hard to shift. Perhaps there was a residue of it in Jonah's complaint that he had been banished from God's sight.

The truth is that Jonah was a fugitive, not an exile. It's ironic that the man who ran a marathon away from God then complained that he had been rejected. Turning away from God takes us into the twilight zone, where our faults are someone else's fault, our rebelliousness can be rationalised and outright sins seem sensible. Adultery is always a tragedy; and it's compounded when the Christian couples who fall into it affirm that God led them there. Deception has triumphed, blinkering them into believing a lie. Let's all pray for ears that hear – and eyes that see.

Let's accept God's discipline when it comes

Prayer: You are the Truth. Bring light and truth to my heart and mind today, Lord. Amen.

Don't snack on camels

BIG PICTURE:
Jonah 2:4
Luke 11:39–44

FOCUS:
'… yet I will look again towards your holy temple.' (Jonah 2:4)

WE HAVE already seen that sin deceives us; ironically, religion can dump us into the dark too. Religious people are often sticklers, meticulous about being right about righteousness. Sadly, sometimes we prioritise issues that are really quite unimportant to God – and ignore what He is passionate about. The Pharisees fussed about theological minutiae and washed their hands before touching the Torah scrolls – yet were happy to bruise their fellow human beings, especially the more spectacular sinners caught in the act. Their spirituality was selective and blinded them to their real deficiencies. The bizarre word picture that Jesus drew of them, desperately trying to fish a tiny gnat out of a drink yet gulping down a huge camel without hesitation (Matt. 23:24), shows how easily we can major on minors and then ignore what really matters.

At first Jonah's prayer about the Temple seems like a pious declaration of hope, but commentators have spotted a possible flaw in his words. Of course, Jerusalem-loving Jonah *would* say that, wouldn't he? His problems all began because his call was not to the comfort and safety of home but rather to the hostile and hated Nineveh. Perhaps it's reading too much into his words, but the white-hot anger that later ignited in Jonah's heart suggests that his repentance was at best fragile and incomplete – which we can all identify with.

Let's avoid a mutated Christianity where we are smugly convinced that God is delighted with us because we can tick a few boxes. Let's ask Him what really matters to *Him* and do what He says.

Prayer: Save me, Lord, from minimising the important and magnifying the insignificant. Amen.

SESSION 2: DAY 5

How to make a fish sick

BIG PICTURE:
Jonah 2:9–10
Matthew 3:1–12

FOCUS:
'And the LORD commanded the fish, and it vomited Jonah onto dry land.' (Jonah 2:10)

IT'S easy to say we are sorry but do nothing about the problem in question. Make no mistake, genuine repentance leads to changed behaviour. This is worth pondering, because I believe that here is the hinge truth that leads so many to live positive, fruitful Christian lives – or wreck everything on the rocks of disastrous decisions. It's so easy to make promises when we are desperate or moved emotionally. But it's follow through and fruit that counts.

I can think of someone I've known distantly for many years, and whenever I see him, he recites the same speech about being in a sin that has trapped him for decades. Thousands of times he has responded with apparent repentance during services. His countless prayers have affirmed that, from now on, his life would be different, that he would finally make good, grace choices and break free from his shackles that have turned rusty with age. Will he die a prisoner of shame still? I fear that he has made that jailhouse his permanent home.

Because Jonah's repentance was so flawed, some commentators believe that the big fish threw up, not only because God commanded it to but because of the nauseating little man in its stomach! It's speculation, but the writer's use of the word 'vomit' here is curious. Jonah isn't spat out but forcibly ejected. One writer says, 'It is no wonder that immediately after Jonah shouts, "Deliverance belongs to Yahweh!" the big fish throws up!' High-sounding speeches and vows that lead nowhere are sickening – to large fish and, more importantly, to God.

> It's easy to make promises ... but it's follow through and fruit that counts

Prayer: Save me, Lord, from excited, emotional moments that lead nowhere. Give me grace and courage to fulfil what I have promised. Amen.

Session 3:
Partnering in the Mission of God

ICEBREAKER:

Have you ever been involved in a Christian project which you were reluctant to join at first? How did it turn out?

FOR GROUP DISCUSSION:

- 'Mission is always about the mobilisation of the imperfect.' How well do you feel that your Christian life thus far has prepared you for sharing your faith? What could you do to improve things?

- Nineveh was a 'hard place'. Do we tend to think of *our* area as hard to reach? Why?

- It's been said that one of the greatest things we can do in mission is to invite people to church so that they can encounter the 'lighthouse community' of God. Do you agree? What should we do to make our services and meetings accessible to those who come?

- How confident are you in your fellow team members when it comes to the work of mission? Spend time praying for people in your church – those who are at the frontline and those who are struggling.

- Jonah expects nothing and yet revival breaks out. Does this mean our expectations are irrelevant to God?

- Mission involves telling. How can we tell people about God without becoming pushy and offensive?

- Mission demands change. Why do we Christians often find change so difficult?

- How do you think your church would do if Nicky the stripper arrived?

PRAYER:

Lord Jesus,
You came.
You spoke.
You lived.
You showed the way.
You suffered.
You died.
You beat death and hell.
Live in us, and through us.
May our lives, our words, our tears, our work
All show and tell the world of Your love.
Amen.

Mission – mobilising the imperfect

BIG PICTURE:
Jonah 3:1
1 Corinthians 1:26–28

FOCUS:
'Then the word of the LORD came to Jonah a second time …'
(Jonah 3:1)

GOD is kinder than most of us can imagine – and we are in need of that kindness more than we think! Part of that liberal goodness is His choosing to use flawed people who are still very much in the process of maturing. Jonah, whose ambition would have been to see the mass incineration of the Ninevites, was himself given another chance, as the word and call of God came once again.

In my earlier years as a Christian, my approach to mission was zealous enough but I was somewhat inept and insensitive in the way that I talked with people about my faith. Yet I'm grateful that God seemed to use even my faltering words to reach others. I was unskilled and occasionally obnoxious, but still people came to faith through my clumsy efforts – and there were many wonderful moments when I knew that a conversation had genuinely helped someone on their life journey. Mission is always about the mobilisation, not of highly trained presenters, but of profoundly ordinary works-in-progress people like us. Biblical history is littered with those who shrank back from their calling because they felt inadequate. But Moses, with his stammering lips (Exod. 4:10–16) and Jeremiah, who felt like a child doing a man's work (Jer. 1:6) were effective anyway – sometimes more effective in weakness (2 Cor. 12:9).

Henry Ward Beecher notes: 'The church is not a gallery for the exhibition of eminent Christians, but a school for the education of imperfect ones.' Feel inadequate for mission? Join the crowd.

Prayer: Lord, help me not to back away from sharing You because of my weaknesses and fears. Use me today. Amen.

Feel inadequate for mission?

SESSION 3: DAY 2

Mission means telling

BIG PICTURE:
Jonah 3:2
Romans 10:1–15

FOCUS:
'... and proclaim to it the message I give you.' (Jonah 3:2)

IT'S a quote that's been used endlessly, particularly in recent years. 'Preach the gospel at all times. If necessary, use words.' The suggestion is that we should live out our faith rather than talk about it; that 'witnessing' for Jesus (as we used to call it) somehow belongs to another darker (and bygone) age.

But I've been in situations where this approach was taken – to little effect. Some churches work hard at serving their communities, are known for their caring and generous hearts – but few seem to come to faith as a result of all their efforts. I'm not suggesting that every action needs to carry a gospel invitation with it, but there are times when we just need to share and speak out the incredibly good news that is the Christian message. God's command to Jonah was precise: head for Nineveh and 'proclaim to it the message I give you.'

And the quote about using words when necessary? It came from the lips of St Francis of Assisi, who is famous mainly for being the patron saint of animals. Converted from a wild life, he gave up every material thing he had, including his clothes, so that he would be totally free to say, 'Our Father in heaven.'

A man of passionate commitment and deep personal spirituality, his life shouted the gospel at high volume. When you've literally given everything up for God, you can rightly imply that words matter less than actions. God told Jonah to speak up; He says the same to all of us.

Prayer: Father, give me words, give me tact, and timing: but let me speak about You. Amen.

Mission means showing

BIG PICTURE:
Jonah 3:3
Titus 3:1–8

FOCUS:
'Jonah obeyed the word of the LORD and went to Nineveh.' (Jonah 3:3)

OUR friends, Christian leaders from America, had spent the weekend speaking to leaders in the UK, and now we were reviewing the event. We asked them what they'd noticed about the people they'd rubbed shoulders with. Both agreed without hesitation that they were stunned by how almost everyone they met was actively engaged in serving their communities. Most had realised that Christianity must be demonstrated as well as spoken (the flip side of our reflection on Day 2 of this section) and so were engaged in working with the homeless, the care and counsel of victims of sexual abuse and rape, serving at drop-in centres for young people or labouring in a host of other practical and creative projects.

Mission calls us to live the message as well as speak it. It was an *obedient* Jonah who went to Nineveh. He called the Assyrians to surrender to God as one who himself was living – for a while, anyway – in the place of surrender. The messenger was part of the message. To quote the animal-loving St Francis again, 'It is no use walking anywhere to preach unless our walking is our preaching.'

Years ago I used to tell people who weren't Christians, 'Don't look at the church, look at Jesus.' I now realise that I was very wrong. First of all, Jesus is invisible and therefore not that easy to look at. Secondly, the church has been created as a working model of kingdom life. God wants people to be able to look at us *and* see Jesus. Let's thank God that it's happening.

Prayer: Thank You, Lord, that the truth is being demonstrated as well as told. Let me be part of that demonstration today. Amen.

SESSION 3: DAY 4

Mission and miracles

BIG PICTURE:
Jonah 3:5
John 11:1–44

FOCUS:
'The Ninevites believed God.' (Jonah 3:5)

WE WERE stunned. My brother-in-law, Chris, had demonstrated complete disinterest (and mild antagonism) to the Christian message. Our children, very young at the time, had talked with him about Jesus, with no effect. We continued to pray. The telephone call came like a bolt out of the blue, as Chris, now a student at Cambridge University, told us that he had made the decision to become a Christian. I dashed upstairs to tell the incredible news to our children, who were pleased but not surprised. Our daughter Kelly asked me an uncomfortable question. 'Why are you so shocked, Dad? We've been praying for him. Didn't you expect *something* to happen?'

The news of the hardened people of Nineveh coming to God is nothing short of shocking. The word used to describe their newfound faith – 'believed' – is the same term in the Hebrew that describes Abraham's relationship with God. And the radical nature of their repentance is a shocker as well. The Assyrians were a most religious people: they shaped their national life according to their belief in the goddess of war, Ishtar. But these people were known to welcome other gods if that would help them get what they wanted – so was this 'turning' for real? Now, as they fast and drape themselves in sackcloth as a sign of mourning and throw themselves on the mercy of the real God, we see what is nothing short of a miracle.

It *is* difficult to pray for some people – especially family members. Their turning would seem absolutely impossible. But the God who can even raise the dead is able.

Prayer: Lord, grant me hope and expectation to see the 'unreachable' reached. Help me to keep asking, and looking out for them. Amen.

Mission's motive

BIG PICTURE:
Jonah 3:1–10
Isaiah 40:1–11

FOCUS:
'When God saw … he had compassion …' (Jonah 3:10)

JONAH'S couldn't-care-less attitude towards the thousands of hapless sinners (now reformed) of Nineveh stands in stark contrast to the tender, gentle heart of God. Our journey so far through this book has shown Him to be both gracious and graceful. Compassion triumphs over judgment, and the punishment that was threatened is cancelled. And all because of God's great love – a theme that runs to the very last verse of this book (Jonah 4:11).

In this third chapter, we see that mission's motive is to care. Evangelism that merely seeks to fill our church buildings with more people is nothing short of heartless expansionism. But when we connect with God's caring heart and begin to see the desperate needs of people who may outwardly appear strong (Nineveh was known as a *very important* city – Jonah 3:3), then our attempts to win people to God through lifestyle and proclamation will be seen to be authentic. People don't want to be 'scalps' that we are collecting or 'souls' that we are winning, and they don't want to be our next project, either. Floyd McClung (who has wonderfully demonstrated his true heart for mission in the choices that he and his family have made) famously said, 'People don't care how much we know. They want to know how much we care.'

Perhaps, like me, you occasionally suffer from compassion fatigue. So overwhelmed by the massive needs of the world, we can retreat. Let's ask the tender-hearted God to give us hearts just like His own.

Prayer: Help me to see the lost as You see them, Lord. Help me to care. Amen.

Perhaps, like me, you occasionally suffer from compassion fatigue

Session 4:
Trusting through Anger and Disappointment

ICEBREAKER:

Have you been, or are you, angry with God? Why? What happened?

FOR GROUP DISCUSSION:

- Jonah was incensed that God had let the murderous Assyrians off. Imagine someone murders a loved one of yours and then becomes a Christian. How would it feel to know that they were forgiven by God?

- 'Anger sometimes comes from unrealistic expectations.' Why do we think that life should be 'good' for those who follow God?

- What are the good reasons for expressing anger? What are the dangers? How can we healthily express our anger to God?

- How can we stand together as a community and profess our faith?

- What is trust?

- Do feelings matter in the walk of faith?

- Our walk with Jesus may include mysteries that we will never fully understand in this life. What mysteries have you faced? What was your response?

- When you are angry and confused, what helps? What doesn't help?
- 'We need God's people.' Why?
- God promises to be with us. What does that mean, and how does that help?

PRAYER:

We come to You, loving Father,
As we are.
To You we come, some with empty hands
That we hoped so much would be full.
To You we come, some with weary souls
We had hoped so much to be strong.
To You we come
With our questions
With our fears
With our anger
With our tears.

We come to You
As we are.
Draw close to us, we pray,
Emmanuel: God with us.
Amen.

SESSION 4: DAY 1

Anger's intensity

BIG PICTURE:
Jonah 4:1
Jeremiah 20:13–18

FOCUS:
'But Jonah was greatly displeased and became angry.' (Jonah 4:1)

JONAH preached one of the shortest (fellow preachers take note) and most successful sermons in the history of preaching and an entire city was rocked to its foundations by the reverberation of revival. You'd think he'd be happy. On the contrary, he was incensed. The writer here is keen for us to know just how upset Jonah was with God.

First of all, there's a literary device used here called a *figura etymologia*. I know that's a mouthful but bear with me. This is a double emphasis used frequently throughout the book of Jonah to show just how intense something was. So the terrified sailors 'feared a great fear' (2x), Jonah was called to 'proclaim the proclamation' (3x) and now he is 'angry with a great anger'. Take it from me. He's upset.

Then there's the use of the word 'great' – a favourite word in this book – Nineveh was a great city, the fish was great, the storm was great – and furious, Jonah's anger was great too. And Jonah's anger was all-consuming – enough to make him ignore God and feel tired of living, even praying for death twice (Jonah 4:3,9).

I've spelt all this out because there are some of us who feel so consumed with rage against God that we are tempted to think there's no way back. The fact that you're reading these words is nothing short of a miracle, because, generally, you and He aren't on speaking terms right now. Know that this white-knuckled man has just been an instrument to shake a city. Count yourself in again.

Prayer: Help me to run to You, and not from You, when frustration fuels my heart. Amen.

SESSION 4: DAY 2

The songs of lament

BIG PICTURE:
Jonah 4:2
Psalm 38:1–22

FOCUS:
'He prayed to the LORD …' (Jonah 4:2)

THERE was an old hymn that we used to sing that included a line that troubled me, as we sang; 'Now I am happy all the day.' There was just one problem with this – I wasn't. Although there are some bright souls who apparently grin their way unceasingly through even the darkest valleys, I don't believe that anyone is permanently thrilled. That's why the songs we sing in worship need to be diverse and not always focused on victory and joy. The heroes of the Bible were certainly not happy all the day; two of the most frequent prayers in the Psalms are 'Why?' and 'How long?'

Perhaps we need to learn to sing songs of lament (although I'm not sure how that works – the worship leader inviting the congregation to 'Stand and sing number 37, *Let's all be fed up together* seems unlikely …). But we can be honest to God in prayer. When I'm sad or angry, my prayers can become little more than speeches. I tell God what I think He wants me to say. When this happens, I sense a yawn in heaven because the Lord is unimpressed by my dishonest babblings (Matt. 6:7).

For all his weakness, Jonah *did* tell God what was really in his heart, even if it was ugly. He brought his frustration into his prayer experience. If you're struggling, depressed, enraged or disappointed, tell God. He knows anyway, but calls us to the intimacy of expressing our pain. As we'll see on Day 3, honesty before God can be a first step to understanding.

Prayer: On darker days, teach me to trust You. When You seem distant, help me pursue You. Amen.

… we can be honest to God in prayer

SESSION 4: DAY 3

Anger and grace

BIG PICTURE:
Jonah 4:2
1 Corinthians 1:18–31

FOCUS:
'I knew that you are a gracious and compassionate God, slow to anger and abounding in love, a God who relents from sending calamity.' (Jonah 4:2)

IT'S ironic that one of the most beautiful descriptions of God found anywhere in the Bible tumbled from the lips of an indignant, enraged man like Jonah. The prophet finally admits why he 'did a runner' from God in the first place – he was afraid that God would be true to His gracious form and forgive the despised Ninevites. God is described as 'gracious and compassionate' (a common pairing in the Old Testament, see Exod. 34:6; Psa. 86:15). And, in contrast to the fuming former fish dweller, God is 'slow to anger'. God 'abounds' in love – a reference to His steady faithfulness. He 'relents from sending calamity'. My friend Gerald Coates affirms that God *does* bring judgment, but that it is His 'strange work.' No wonder Paul describes the work of Christ on the cross as a 'scandal'.

But Jonah is so mad with rage that he just can't stand God. So why should anyone complain about such beauty and grace? The answer is simple. We want God to be gracious and forgiving to *us* – but not to paedophiles, serial killers like Ted Bundy (who made a profession of faith just before his execution), former concentration camp guards – or anyone at all that we dub our enemy. And we want God to fix the evil in the world – but the idea that He might rush to smite us when we step out of line is less palatable. God *is* good – scandalously so.

Prayer: Thank You for Your grace to me. Help me celebrate when You are gracious to others. Amen.

SESSION 4: DAY 4

Anger takes us back three chapters

BIG PICTURE:
Jonah 4:3
Job 19:1–29

FOCUS:
'Now, O Lord, take away my life, for it is better for me to die than to live.' (Jonah 4:3)

TALK about ingratitude! A Yahweh-controlled fish saved Jonah's life – and now his repeated prayer is for death. The reason for his suicidal tendency was the nature of God. Jonah couldn't face serving someone who would do the kind of things that God was doing. Oblivion was more inviting.

This is stubbornness to the extreme – but it also shows that, in a way, Jonah has learned very little. He still wants to run away – but this time, he looks to flee not to a distant country but to the grave.

Unresolved anger has a disabling effect on our lives, strangling hope, tripping us up and sentencing us to wander in endless circles, experiencing little or no growth. And it causes us to forget even the most vivid lessons that should be with us forever. You would think that Jonah's trip through storms and fish guts would have provided him with a lasting education. But now he's back to square one. He's heard the call of God twice but he is 'ever hearing but never understanding ... ever seeing but never perceiving' (Acts 28:26).

Perhaps you've been knocked down by anger for too long. You've watched, even enviously, as others have gone further in God than you. Sometimes you've almost resented those brand new Christians with their bright, hopeful faith. Maybe you've even wished that life itself would end, because it's all too much.

Please think again. Don't run from God but come to Him with your protests. Learn from your past and take the first step towards a better tomorrow.

Prayer: I want to learn and grow, Lord. Take me forward. I choose progress again. Amen.

Talk about ingratitude!

SESSION 4: DAY 5

How will we end?

BIG PICTURE:
Jonah 4:1–11
Matthew 16:13–20

FOCUS:
'Should I not be concerned about that great city?' (Jonah 4:11)

WE LIKE God to give us answers – but sometimes He nudges us towards the truth by asking us poignant questions. Jesus wanted to ease His disciples towards understanding, and so asked them, 'Who do you say I am?' (Matt. 16:15).

The Lord was looking for a spokesperson, and so hinted at Isaiah with His question: 'Whom shall I send? And who will go for us?' (Isa. 6:8). Isaiah got the hint – much faster than Jonah.

When it was time to stop Saul's bloodletting campaign against the Christians, and turn him into Paul the apostle, it all started with a question: 'Saul, Saul, why do you persecute me?' (Acts 9:4).

Now, the book of Jonah ends with God putting a penetrating question to His ever-pouting prophet: 'Should I not be concerned …?'

Jonah's reply is not recorded. Perhaps he ignored the question – he'd done that before (Jonah 4:4–5) when he walked out of revival town. Did Jonah ever humble himself and give in, ending the wrestling match with God for good? When we met him, he was a runner – not an auspicious beginning. So what of his ending – would he fight tooth and nail to his last breath? The question was intended to prompt Jonah towards a good finish.

Recently, I boarded a flight to attend the funeral of a good friend, Sue Scott. A wife and mother of two children, she fought cancer with courage and faith. Martin, her husband, was able to write 'She died well.' She finished well. May we be like her.

> 'Should I not be concerned about that great city?'

Prayer: May I run the race to win, and finish my life well. With Your grace, it can be so. Amen.